a gift for

from

Editorial Director: Todd Hafer
Editor: Jeff Morgan
Art Director: Kevin Swanson
Designer: Michelle Nicolier
Production Art: Dan Horton

Printed and bound in the U.S.A.

ISBN: 1-59530-136-4
First Edition, March 2006

10 9 8

BOK2065

# cats

antics & attitudes

GIFT BOOKS

from Hallmark

OK. Let's get this straight.
My name is not Fluffy-Wuffy.

Yo, dog!
Yeah, you, bonehead.
Can't get me, can ya?
Na-na-na-na-na!

You know we raise hell,
but you can never catch
us in the act.

I hung in there 'till I couldn't hang no more.

OK. OK. So I've got a tiny anger management problem.

I thought you knew
the way to the litter box.

Just step back from
my chair slowly....

Look into my eyes...
you are feeling drowsy...
so drowsy...you will buy
the fillet of sole...you will....

I'm waiting for a lap here!

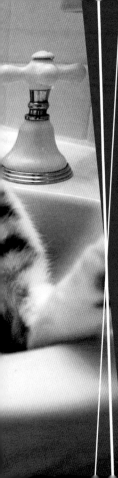

Hey! Do I look at you
when you're in the bath?
Oh. Right.

What part of
"I am the center of the universe"
do you not understand?

My perm is ruined!

Let's see. It says, "...the cat is the noblest creature...." So true. So true.

One day, Goldie, one day....

So much for the
economy beach vacation!

...then when the mice come
to tell Santa what they want,
Santa gets what he wants.

Please come back—
I can't help it if I
have tuna breath!

Hmmm. Am I purring,
or is this one of those
"Magic Fingers" vibrating beds.

This hot tub is defective.

Uh, if you want me on a low-fat diet, just bring me skinny mice, OK?

Having shredded the curtains and upholstery, I extend my paw in an adorable gesture of reconciliation.

Oh sure,
a dog can bring in the paper...
I can sort the mail.

Just because the furniture is already ugly, don't think that I won't ruin it.

I'm going to the store
for catnip. Anybody need
anything while I'm out?

I just love what I've
done with this place.

When you rule the world,
anywhere you sit is a throne.

Ready! Set! Shred!

About your socks....

**WHAT?!**
**You forgot the salmon again?**

I'm giving myself a time-out
for what I left on your pillow.

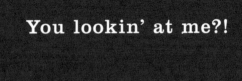

Just call me Flossie.

Please! Please! Please!
Open the door.
I gotta go bad!

How would they like it if I put a cage around their snacks?

When you want to accessorize
with style, take the cat.

OK, now how do you do that
Cat's Cradle thing?

No matter what you've done,
blame it on the dog.

It's amazing what you'll wear when you've had too much catnip at a party.

You want this chair?
Well, talk to the paw,
cuz the face ain't listening.

Hey, where's your copy of
THE CAT IN THE HAT?

Come a little closer.
I need a scratching post.

You don't want to know where I've been licking!

These shirts are perfect—
medium on the starch,
heavy on the cat hair.

Yeah. Yeah. I hear ya,
but I'm not comin'
until you say please.

Humans: Your ignorance baffles me and makes me tired at the same time.

What do you have to do
around here to get a refill?

If you have enjoyed this book,
Hallmark would love
to hear from you.

Please send comments to
Book Feedback
2501 McGee, Mail Drop 215
Kansas City, MO 64141-6580

or e-mail us at:
booknotes@hallmark.com